SEASONS of a
SEWER GIRL

Acclaims for Dawn P. Harrell

Dawn's writing is truly a work of art. Her imagery is like an artist painting a masterpiece with beauty and boldness. She doesn't hold back as she spills the ink from the depths of her soul. She has no fear in expressing her emotions. She writes of how life can be messy, but also how messy can be beautiful. Dawn shows how vulnerability is turned into strength, which is rare in this world today. You can't help hanging onto every word written and crave the next line. You will feel the words pierce your heart as they draw you in deeper. Seasons of a Sewer Girl will transport you into her world, and you'll journey through the seasons of life, love, loneliness, hope, and everything in between.

April Y. Spellmeyer

There are very few moments when ink becomes spilled whispers of a soul in seasons of process. This book is exactly that; a soul on the journey of raw breathing. If you have ever found yourself waist-deep in the sewage of life, wading through the muck and processes of cleaning off labels, fears, and rising again, this is a must-read.

Avant Avant-garde

I have always loved reading. I love getting lost in the words and letting my mind go wherever the words take me. Not so long ago, I happened upon the writings of Dawn Harrell. I instantly felt connected to this woman whom I have never met. Her talk of healing and growth hit home for me. It made me feel things I didn't know I needed to feel. Some poetry makes you realize your own strength; some helps you realize just how much you need to heal. Great poetry makes you feel both. For me, the works of Dawn Harrell definitely have both and then some.

Emily James

Dawn P. Harrell is a talented and passionate poet. Her writing is brilliant, evocative, and heartfelt. Not only are her words relatable, but they are a portal to our own depths within.

Kristin Kory

SEASONS of a SEWER GIRL

a collection of poetry and prose by

Dawn P. Harrell

300 SOUTH MEDIA GROUP

NEW YORK | UNITED STATES

ISBN-13: 978-0-9970356-5-0

First Printing June 2021
Published by 300 South Media Group

Book Design & Layout | 300 South Media Group | 300SMG.COM

*In memory of my Mamaw, Rosa, you always
showed me what unconditional love was,
no matter the season. You taught me to be strong.
I hope I'm half the woman you were someday.*

*You always wanted me to write a book,
so this one's for you.*

CONTENTS

Foreword

Dawn has a beautiful way of pouring her heart out with words, telling a story we can all relate to, using poetry and prose to paint a picture that helps us feel less alone. She's been there, and her words grab your hand to let you know that someone else has walked the same path and you're going to be okay. Dawn's writing is unique because it's not the same words we see over and over, written differently. Her words are from a place where good things still exist; honesty, kindness, but most of all, her words are surrounded by a light you don't see much anymore. Dawn's words are capable of pulling you out of the darkness to show you some light and let you know there's hope; there's always hope. Even when you don't see any, her words will lead you there.

Stephanie Bennett-Henry

Acknowledgments

To my parents, my boys, my family – some days you are the reason I hold it all together, and I'm grateful for that. Thanks for loving me through all my highs and lows and the days in between.

Jay, my most constant friend, and always up for my late-night thoughts. Thanks for all the writing advice and help through the years, but more importantly, your awesome friendship.

Stephanie, nothing I can ever say would have you thinking less of me. Our friendship is so easy, and I'd not have a page at all without you pushing me to believe in my work.

Sabrina, the best friend a girl could have. Thanks for always calling me out when I need it and answering no matter what.

Jake, often my muse, always my rock, you believe in me even when I don't and calm the storm inside. Thanks for being my home when I need one.

Deanna, how would we make it through the day without our banter? Thanks for always checking in on me, friend.

My sisters and friends in the writing community, so blessed you're in my life. April, Emily James, Avant, and Kristin thanks for your help with this book.

To my friends and followers--thanks for reading my words and letting me know how you feel. My wish is that no matter what you go through, you will have hope as we weather the seasons together.

SEASONS of a SEWER GIRL

Season of Darkness

Been a long time since I felt almost alright with being me. So many days with crushing fear and despairing for what could come next. Now in my silence, I can sit alone and sort the pieces in my mind, and what I find is that what I was told were lies. The monster actually was not ever me.

I gained my independence the moment you hurt anyone but me. I wish now I would have valued myself more, but I couldn't see then. Now I know my worth, and you will never take my freedom again.

Just when I thought you knew me, I felt the softness slip and caught a glimpse of shiny scales. You wrap your black velvet lies in a cloak of comfort perfectly. The warmth I felt, an illusion to what end? You feed your ego with loyalty, but the one you didn't count on was me. Bested by the one you thought was weak, leaving me stronger from the lies meant to break me.

Loving you was killing me slowly. Starts off small, with something to "help" you be better, so you don't see it coming. So busy trying to accommodate your love, you miss the signs. Merely a distraction that you miss because you don't play games. When did love get so complicated? I guess when it became all about you. That's the kind of love I'm better off without.

The mystery in you was the key to your effortless seduction of me. You cast a shadow wide enough for me to step inside and revel in the dark unknown. Sinking in the pool of your eyes, made the pain ephemeral, so I'd forget and fall too many times in what I thought was love from an emotional vampire.

Worked so hard and put back all the pieces.
The missing ones I crafted from kindness and
gentle hugs along the way. Some mortar
slipped and let dust in the cracks. It's so fine
you almost can't see it at first; a hint to
change yourself, disguised as helpful.
Thoughts planted that you've forgotten
what's been said. Tiny needling chips that
chink the armor, and suddenly you're
bleeding, remembering who I've become and
the reasons for the mortar. I'm still grateful
for the kindness of those who remind me
who I am and pick up the pieces and dust
away the sand when I'm weak, and I forget
not to let you in.

Yours was the last of the relationships that left me haunted by your opinion of who I should be. So many rules, lists, pedantic ways that I should act and love and become. I truly was still becoming when I knew you, and I'm grateful your standards were twisted enough to show me I was okay. In some ways, you helped 'cause I know what way I never want to be. I'm loving my own clumsy, insecure, sometimes inappropriate, trying new things me.

Season of Depression & Anxiety

Creeps in like a dark tide, the thoughts that tie me down. I'll be content for a moment, but it always seeps back in. Words inside me that beg to be unleashed. Sometimes I'm afraid to let them go. They soothe my strangled heart like a poison.

Freed up a little space in the chaos of my thoughts for a break. Sometimes in the ebb and flow of constant flood, I stop catching my words, I can't string them together, and I feel frozen in place. My emotions spur me on, though, never retreating; they fuel my fire. The depth of what I feel keeps me always together and pairs well with the melancholy cloak that shrouds me still.

Glimpses of hope sprinkled through the day sometimes leave me frozen. So accustomed to rainy days, I don't trust the sun. I can see brighter things from the veil of darkness that hangs over me, but I can't bring myself to lift it and step outside. On the days I join the ones with the sun on their faces, I feel so warm but exposed. Maybe someday I'll come out to stay. For now, just the thought leaves me frozen.

Gloomy days my mind betrays me. Tells me
things I've long reconciled. Sparks doubts I
thought were gone. Looks at me as if a
stranger I've become, and I have long shed
the broken, shattered, scared, and tired shell
I was. Stronger, lighter, less fearful, almost
confident as the days wear on. Not the girl I
was but one healing; a stranger picking up
jagged pieces, fitting each back till I'm
a semblance of whole.

How do you make it through okay? Pushing back the tears that threaten, swallowing pleas for help that sound like whining. Why do we have to be so tough? I often spend my days this way in hopes my fortitude will shut it off. But the feelings build like a crescendo to boiling, and I'm sure if someone had time to look into them, my eyes would betray me. But they don't. And I have another day to wonder if this will be the one that parts of me leak out onto the ground, leaving me messy.

I didn't even see you coming today. I pictured a day like any other without you breaking in to tell me what I am lacking, without the claws of doubt scraping down my spine. The effort to put you back inside is sometimes overwhelming, yet here we are again, my ever-present companion. Slipping out from behind that smile that tried to reach my eyes.

I search for a better way to stave off the
bitter chill of melancholy. I've never been
one for maudlin, much too closed to let
anything escape. The words I pen give sweet
relief for moments of curious reflection. The
chance of better days brings warm tears to
my cheek when I'm alone; gives me hope
that soon my face can be lit up with
a grin again.

I'm ever out in search of things that give me a
respite from the shuddering in my mind.

It claws its way to the surface ever so often, that tugging, unworthy feeling I tuck so deep. Usually, when I'm feeling a smile or accomplished, it tears its way to stifle my happiness one more time. Were I ever to feel good enough to deserve this life of late, could I actually keep it for myself, or is that just not my fate? This crawling thing within me doesn't hurt as it once did, so maybe there's still hope for me in my days. God knows I've paid a thousand times over so I could finally feel free to be me.

It never stops, the constant flood of syllables
flowing through my mind like a roaring river
mostly, sometimes a melodic trickle like an icy
creek. Were I strong like a tree with deep
roots, there would be a hollow for the things
to escape that dwell in me to overflowing
and keep me ever from the silence, which
might be my favorite melancholy.

It visits from time to time, that slowly enveloping dread. I tell myself I know who I am, but that doubt covers me in an oily puddle. Makes the strongest unsure when it lays your soul bare, seemingly for all to see. Would I ever find a way to beat it, I wonder would I miss the haunting or finally find a way to rest within this skin?

It washes over me in waves, the panic. Sometimes I even wake up to it, trying to breathe and imagine warm water washing over me instead of unknown terror. Some like me deal with it privately, so we don't recognize each other to throw out a lifeboat. Hope you always feel your breaths calming, and not like water. Hope the minutes don't last for an eternity. Hope one day you and me will break free from the panic.

It's cold outside, and I'm trying to brave this
season. So many shiny, happy baubles
decorating everything in sight. I look for the
warmth of the glow they cast to ignite a little
song in my soul. Maybe the shimmering
lights could add a twinkle to even my eyes.
But I'm still drawn to the mosses that hang
from my bones and the darkest time of night.
Can you love the way I make it anyway? I'm
still giving, its just pieces from my
not so festive heart.

It's dark so early and so late. An extra chill in
my soul. Winter's calling. There's a hush in
the air. I miss the nighttime songs. Extra
sadness in my bones while winter's calling.
Can you feel the frosty sting?
My winter's calling.

It's Fall here. Never really know what to think about Fall. The beautiful colors falling to the ground distract from the death taking place all around. The chill seems to blow away the haze and the days seem crisper, quieter. Even the sunsets seem to paint a little deeper, reminders of Persephone's demise, but you can't see it for the boldness of the changing seasons. I get distracted, so I forget why my days are tinted a deeper shade of melancholy, and my losses seem heavier. No one is painting bright the flowers for a while, and I'm here feeling the chill.
Fall is here in me.

It's harder on some days. Have to hold everything together even when it gets heavy, and I'm tired. Always have two looking up to me, seeing how I handle things, relying that I'll never falter. They are why I can still be brave. No matter how impossible things get to looking in front of me, nothing can beat me 'cause I will always be their rock, and that in itself keeps me brave.

My old friend insomnia is in bed with me again. I spend my endless nights thinking about the things I wish I were, not browsing deep within the chambers of my soul to glimpse how far I've come. I was so insecure when you saw me last. I let others crush my soul. I'm strong enough, yet still, I'm stacking bricks where my stained-glass heart used to glow.

On nights I feel my heart could burst from the thoughts inside my head. I wish I could see into the mystic and leave my mind behind. To be that free, to fly unhinged, to love without fear of tomorrow. That bliss seems unreachable, but I fight on and reach out when I can; upon the chance it could really be true.

On these raw days when I feel much more
inadequate than usual like I'm walking around
without skin, I dream what it would be like to
walk so tall and believe anything is possible.
So I close my eyes and I wait.

I've always tried to give my all, whatever I was doing. Been a bit of a perfectionist, doling out pieces of myself to anyone who seemed to need it. I was too busy to see it doesn't work like that. Someone, something gets only the best, and others are slighted or forgotten entirely, like me. Didn't think to give myself the same courtesy until I started running out of pieces.

So much. I think I'd like it to stop. The fluttering in my chest even when things go well. My silent partner telling me it's not enough, even when it is. But nothing is easy; not sure I'd trust it if it were. My melancholy days, I know what I am and wear the feeling like a cloak. Tonight, I close my eyes with a smile to end a successful day. My mind snaps me awake with doubts before I even enjoy the grin, but do I regret it? Nothing is easy.

So much of what goes through my mind is a toss-up of emotions. Were you to have tea leaves, voodoo, or the like, we could never predict the swings within that keep my soul astir. Some days I wish for quiet, a brief respite from the churning, but then who would I be? It's a haunting mystery, but for now, I'm complacent just being me.

Some days I see them clearly, and some days not at all; the little monsters creeping through my halls. I think I'm doing fine; a facade like everything is great, and then here they come, out for show, lining my transgressions up in a row. I wish they would stay hidden so no one else could see the burdens that I carry and things that bother me.

Some days my heart can run the gamut of emotions, despairing so in the early hours to a vibrant ray of hope in the night. I get so close to freedom from this cage I keep my soul in. I stand behind the bars and feel the sun and rain and wind on my face, and I wonder what the other side is like. But my comfort is holding the bars from the inside, so I swallow my hope and settle in; so close.

Some nights I close my eyes and feel the sun on my face. Warm breezes, the smell of cut grass, sweat on my skin. Beautiful days I wanted never to end. Memories swell in my heart and take some of the sting from the aches I carry, reminding me how to grin when I forget. Those days seemed so long, didn't they? Guess I needed them to be to outlast these seasons without the sun.

Some nights I wake barely breathing, a rush of panic for unknown things I've failed at through the day. Becoming pretty good at swallowing the panic and settling back in so I can face the coming hours. You might see me weary or torn about what to do, but the girl who stares back at you from my eyes will always live her truth.

This thunder that rumbles inside me, I try so hard to count away the time so it won't spark. It's always churning below the surface different shades of grey, some days wispy, misty, chokingly thick. It feeds on all the hurts I bring within. I've never known where else to take them. Storms wrapped up in my eyes, begging to call in the tides, but I keep it still because it's mine. There's comfort in the rolling clouds I keep buried in the thunder inside.

There are days I feel like I almost can ride the sky with a burst of feeling, content in the path that I follow no matter how rocky the road. Then there are days I feel the destruction of who I want to be raining down on me with an urgency that seeps deep into my bones. Whatever the day, I know there's another coming. What it will be has a lot to do with me. I never give up, although sometimes the grins are fleeting. I'm secure in the hope birthed out of all I've witnessed thus far. Another night is coming to drape me in the stillness of the stars.

There have been times paralyzed, sleeping, or staring through the dark moments; time I did the best I could but can't get back. I've grown through the pain, lost moments but not wasted. As still at times, the words won't form to bleed it out for me. We do our best. It is enough, and so are you.

This version of me that you see, I wish I could glance it for a moment. You always think I am so strong when inside I tremble at the days. So many things I'd love to claim as my own, yet inside there is a haze of dust and cobwebs long forgotten. I won't dare show a crack. Once the wear starts to show, it's a helluva thing to try and put everything back.

Those days I struggle just to get out of bed, they seem so long. Sometimes they come in a row, and I'm scared they won't end. So tired, like a blanket of sadness so heavy telling you give in and just sleep. I reach out anyway, every time. Not having what it takes to give in, I'm always amazed when the shadow recedes, and I feel the warmth of the sun. And even the dreary days are beautiful when you come back. So always come back. I'll always be back too, waiting for you.

Today I thought about the things you do to look put together. For a moment, it made me sad. Then I remembered that's your choice. So much I relate to the anomalies, so refreshing, but the ride is not easy. Sometimes I ache to my core from feeling so much and grow weary and leak tears. But this is how we were made, and oh what I'd miss were I not an anomaly.

Wish I could tell you I write because I love it. Sometimes it's just not that way. Feeling so much, thoughts churning all the time. At times, the words just claw at your chest to get out when there's no more room. You write to get some relief, to sort it on the paper and hope some of it makes sense. Sometimes it does, sometimes even to someone else. Then room to exhale and begin again.

Season of Heartache

Don't try to climb down to where I am; it's not what you think. I may seem intriguing at a glance, but you don't know my depths. We'll do the dance and try to connect until you catch a glimpse of me, and the shiny wears off of what you thought I could be, and it's just me. So don't' climb down to where I am; let me keep my foolish heart.

Felt the ice in my soul crack a little as of late. So many emotions run through me, sometimes like a lazy river cracking the resolve I have set. Seems like a little break can cause a huge web of pain to seep through the wall I've so carefully constructed but isn't that the way it goes? The fissure will form whether we mean to feel or not. There's no way to stop a breaking heart, an overflow of feeling. The heat of depression radiating inside. So many things to try and thaw what you have built. And I feel better from what I most fear, every time. Maybe we should be a little more willing to see the feelings flow.

Have a minute to think since I left. At first, I
thought I just never was enough for you.
Now with some distance, it becomes clearer,
all the hurdles you wanted me to jump
through. It would have only taken a bit of
courage from you to stand up and say I was
what you wanted. But you didn't, and I'm
gone, and for once I'm the one with the
courage leaving you 'cause I'm better
on my own.

I could never really be what you wanted, so I guess I just quit trying. So many days trying to fit into a mold, not my shape, to make you happy. I don't blame you. Lord knows I had my struggles with myself to think that would make you love me. Now things have changed. I do love me. So take the rules and restrictions and impart them to another helpless soul. I know who I am and who I was meant to be, and none of that fits into your plans for me. I'm out the door. I'm free. Hate you couldn't just let me be...me.

I long for you in the moments I am weak. I know you aren't good for me. Not sure I'm good for anyone, but I still dream deep in the night when I am most myself. I hope someday you'll find what it was you needed. Maybe I'll find someone who needs me. I want to deserve that, not the ache from not being the one you thought I should be.

I say what needs to be said. Sometimes it's
just not what you want from me. But I've had
lies blown in my face so long I can't say
anything else but my truth and survive. I'd
rather be alone than have to tread lightly and
dilute the fact I can't be all you need. So go
find some pretty little lies. The best of me lies
only in the honesty I can't bear to
live without.

I tried so hard to give you what you needed. Hard to fill another from an empty vessel. The things you need I've never had for myself, so I don't know how to give them to you. Remembering why now I am alone, when you aren't given, you don't learn how to take care of another. Patience to teach comes at a price too high.

I try to approach each love with a spirit of giving, slowly learning it is not what my heart blinds itself to. Can you see the tears fall and burst and shatter? Colored pieces bleed the dreams I thought would matter, swept away, discarded, left washed away, and scattered.

If you knew the depth of the feelings in me, you could never mistake me for hollow. You find me cold, but that's not because I am. I uncurl these vines guarding my heart for only the persistent gardener. Maybe move on down to a forest where the path is clear.

I'm spinning a web to catch those parts of me that falter and move away from who I long to be; no more victim to my weaknesses. I pray I'm growing stronger every step I take. Don't try to catch me. I'm on my own and doing fine. Best you can do is crawl right out of my mind.

Lie to me just a few moments longer. I'll pretend you're going to stay. Tell me I'm worth the risk. I'll pretend you think I am. The truth sometimes weighs so much. It's nice to close your eyes and rest in the dream. So tell me again how much I mean to you, still, and I'll feel the grin starting and the butterflies once more.

Priority means different things to so many. In my heart, I made you one, swept out the cobwebs, and shined everything up for you. But our ideas were different, and you left when you felt so much better. And I'm here less of a priority than ever, watching the webs grow back.

So many ways to say the things I feel, but I keep them hidden inside. I'd never want to be a burden, I tell myself, but sometimes I wonder if that's kind of a lie. So many times, I've bled out the pain only to have it used against me later. After you keep it a while, the feelings can ache in your chest, but I can still bleed onto the pages. Who do you tell your secrets to? I pray you have someone or that you can pray them away.

Some nights it hurts to breathe when the tears won't stop, and I know I'm just not enough. God, I want to be! I try so hard, but you can't give what you don't have, I guess. Keep fooling myself into believing I could be what you need instead of pain, but it's in my veins, and I can't bleed it out or cry it out. So I'm bound to my shadows and the haunting memories of when I made you smile.

The things I was told about myself still haunt my thoughts some days. Too much, too little, too everything; lucky anyone would want me. I am lucky now; several seasons have passed. I can be lots of things, and I am, on any given day, but who I am is okay. The remnants of that girl, they hardly resemble me now, and I love us both, and I want me for now.
That is enough.

There were always moments. They flash by me when I try to sleep and pop up in the worst and best of times. I never knew how much you meant until they were what I was left with. Sometimes we see things as a whole, and the moments tinkle to the floor and get swept away. Some days I try to piece them together and feel you with me again, if only for a few moments.

Thought you were different, but you aren't.
Maybe me just making things so
uncomplicated seals my fate. I can listen, I
can comfort, but then you're all patched up
and gone, and I'm left alone to clean up the
mess with a heart drained of compassion and
a gaping hole where my confidence used to
live. Maybe next time, I'll be wiser,
but not likely.

★ · ◆ · ★

Throw up the no vacancy sign on this heart of mine. The damages wrought here have left me feeling condemned. I'd love to fix it up for you, but the costs would be too great. It's ready for the wrecking ball. I'm sorry, you came too late.

What I wanted, I've never really said out loud until it's been too late. Do we have to say the things, does giving them a voice make them more necessary or important? I wanted you to say something, anything, about how you cared or didn't. I wanted to hear something about your day and not just the weather. I wanted, needed, to hear it, but it's too hard, and I'm gone, looking for a voice with bravado to just speak to me, and maybe then I'll be bold enough to say...

Why did you give your love so freely and then begin to take it back? Just to give enough to have me trust you. Just enough to shake these carefully constructed defenses. Did you think I'd keep pouring my soul in the cracks and watch it run out on the floor? So take it back, what pieces you gave, I can't take less than all anyway.

Without you, I always seem to find my step a little bit unsteady, even when I hold my head high and pretend I've just got it all together. Without you, my blues seem greyed and nights are too short, and my mind... Without you, my mind is on red. Can't get you out of my head, but here I am trying... without you.

Wonder what it would have been like for you just to have risked a fall. It's like you reach that place every time where you turn your back on it all. My fault for always following. My heart doesn't seem to shut off hope. It'd be like snowfall in Mississippi if you ever let me see behind the stoic gaze that holds me frozen here once more.

You always counted me out as among the fallen, never coming down far enough to see what you'd become. Now I'm thriving here in the shadows, and from the pedestal you made yourself, I bet it's cold up there alone.

You said you wanted to be with me. The words start out innocuous. So easy to fall into step when you're on that high of new infatuation. What you find later, especially if you're a lover of words, is that everyone doesn't hold them in the esteem that you do. Words are your breath. To some, they are a means to an end, the end of you and what you believed to be truth. Because words... how could they be used for ill gain? And this is why a writer's heart has to learn all the ways words can be misconstrued and leave your heart in pieces on the ground.

You were the one who always thought I deserved better. So many days have passed since then. I think back and notice you were the one who wanted the best for me. Isn't that what love is - wanting the very best for someone else, no matter what? So I'm sorry for letting you go thinking it was about me. It never really was, was it? It was about what you and I deserved to be....together.

Season of Hope

I'm becoming a ghost of who I used to be. Timid and afraid, unsure of all my steps as if a mistake would destroy me. Somewhere along my path, I shed the ones who kept me fearful, and now I feel a welling of hope where the fear had made a home. I'm a ghost of who I used to be, but that shaky wisp of a girl, though I learned so much from her, was never meant for me.

Another year has begun. More chances to dig in and be what you want, but don't we have those all the time? Day by day, I move through it all with thoughts of such improvement. Sometimes holding on to get through another night is success enough. To you, who feel the days without a grand gesture aren't enough – you made it. I'm so proud of you. Now let us go off to tackle another… together.

There can be oceans of hurts inside your soul. Gullies washed open by tears you didn't even know you cried. Some come fresh to your mind and often, reminding you of some perceived failure or misstep you may have made. Mocking your resolve to get better, wanting to drag you back down. Some just a feeling of sadness that you can't find a reason for throughout the day. Some like me learn to live this way, taking almost comfort in the sadness. Seems better on some days than clawing back to the way things used to be. I still go there in the deep hollows of my mind. But I'm learning that I can find a way to fill in some of the holes. Maybe get out and walk and feel the sun warming my face. Some days I can, and it's magic. Take care of me even if I don't feel like it. Baby steps.

Can you grab a shovel and fill in the holes of that gully with the shame and guilt that was never really yours to bear? Bury it building a foundation of love for the things you forgot gave you meaning?

Some days I can't. But now I'm okay with that. Days like today, I'm feeling the tears behind my eyes and willing them not to come. As I look out on a beautiful yard covered in a dusting of colored leaves, and feel grateful.

Let's get up and find some hope. Keep burying those things you weren't meant to have. There is meaning in the glimmers we see of who we were meant to be, and it's beautiful, and you so deserve it.

Who can you be when you indulge yourself to dream of galaxies and garnets, beautiful kisses, and bright eyes pouring love into your own? A success you thought unattainable. Misty rain washing your soul clean on a warm starlit night. Or is it something else to you? And who's to say it has to stay just a dream.

I love the ones who bring a little strange, something I wasn't expecting, a passion I never noticed to be real and raw despite the risks. Everyone is so busy trying to fit in. I want a body that stands out, someone strange like me.

I often look for that place inside where I don't feel compelled to wear what the world lays out for us today. Where beauty breathes without falter and you and me without the insecurities that hold us miles apart. I close my eyes and breathe in the thought and pray you'll meet me there someday.

I see how well you carry on day by day with
the weight of the world barely visible from
that smile that always reaches your eyes. I
wonder what it takes to be so strong. As I
move through the days balking at shadows,
sometimes paralyzed by my fear of just
deciding which way to go. Your strength
bolsters me to be all I was meant to be when
I let it; what a precious gift to loan out to a
soul shaky like me.

I'm learning. Still, the broken parts of me form the foundation of who I am meant to be. We sometimes mistake our strength for chinks in the armor when nothing could be further from the truth. The mosaic stained by all the tears we've cried, a beautiful picture still in the making. I hope we see how lovely it is someday.

On the days when you feel bested by the weight of the things you carry, remember the reasons you live the way you do; most days spent in solitude trying not to burden another, often misconstrued as callous instead of care. Tears washing away the fractures of your image cracked again. Unnecessary ritual, maybe. You know who you are, and it is beautiful.

Saw a sliver of light peeking through my defenses. I thought it would terrify me, but instead, it warmed my face. The heart yearns for the things the mind says will create havoc in our lives, but will they really? I guess the fear of trying could be the worst part; if I let you see what's in me.

So many things I wish I would have seen
when I was younger and full of dreams. I've
pressed my memories of relationships in the
pages of my journals like flowers, thankful
they go there to die so I can live this life with
beautiful dreams of a healthy love or even
just peace alone. I deserve that;
pressed memories.

Sometimes I need to step back and let the world fall away. Punchdrunk from all the responsibility weighing me down, I close my eyes and feel the breeze on my face, and for a moment, I am free, setting down even what's not mine to carry so once again
I can be me.

The days are growing lighter, shadows becoming shorter. I'm growing longer roots now and not so afraid of blowing over. Some of the time is still spent just moment to moment moving forward, but on days like this, I feel like I am thawing from within.

Some days I still feel like the little girl who lost her mother and tried to pick up where her Mom left off to keep from shattering. Wish I would have known back then how many ways there were to shatter. Maybe I'd have known sooner that it's okay that all of the pieces don't fit quite like they did before.

Everyone is not going to love the way you love. Some days the physical bruises hurt less than the ones in your mind. You got away. Then you relearn how to live a little differently, as you had to rearrange the pieces that were left. And you feel the wind blow through the cracks and chill your resolve to build that better life. But still, you rise, maybe not every day but most. But it becomes alright cause you become easier on yourself. And bit by broken bit it happens, you feel good in your skin, sometimes out of nowhere, a grin. That little girl is still there, but you are there for her now, and there's hope in the shattering.

Thinking of you tonight and the burdens you
carry each day, so strong and with such
grace. Helping others like you always do.
Never setting down the load. Afraid maybe
you can't lift it again. That's surely just my
thought. You never know you make a
sacrifice, giving yourself without measure.
The brightest soul I think I've ever seen.

Where do you go inside when you already feel
buried upon waking? Tears welling up over
coffee, and you don't know why. Sometimes
I can't find a place. Heart out on display
through no choice of mine, but I can feel the
beating in my blood. Just the thought of it
awakens me from my shroud. Picturing dark,
rich war paint coursing through my veins. All
the days gone to battle, and still, here we are.

Can you feel it? One more day is inside you,
and tomorrow is yet to come.

It's trying to get cold outside, my favorite kind of grey days. They calm the storm inside me, more than any kind of sunny can. The winter's eve approaching leaves a hint of coffee and biting cold. Something different to awaken the magic of the season. To brush your face and make you feel alive; winter's eve.

Wonderful to spend some time in the garden
of your thoughts. Not the ones we pick up
along the way of doubt and insecurity, the
cool ones that make you want to languish in a
sea of moss and watch the butterflies. The
ones that stretch a grin across your face while
the sun warms your skin. The ones that make
you stay a little longer, 'cause it feels so good
to just be. Wishing all the time,
this could be me.

Season of Loneliness

And what if love is not meant for me? I've wasted too many years, too many tears on the ones not meant for me. Turned my blind eye to the advantages taken against my love that didn't deserve to be given. Done with sharing parts of my soul with those who'd misplace and stomp the pieces into the ground. I'm loving me more. So if it's not meant for me, this blood that's quick in my veins will sing the song of solitude that shall render me whole at last. Free to be me.

Can't get close enough anymore to let you
see the depths of the feelings that roil in me.
Salty tears churning turbid emotions. Praying
the dam will hold the drops so close not one
would fall. An ocean ever changing within.
Warm no matter the cold it's living in. Still, I
crash just like the waves upon the shore.
Wearing down my resolve once more.

So many times, I fall into relationships not right for me, especially in love. I try to set boundaries for protection. They are chipped away by loneliness and clever words even though my heart screams "do not pass." There I am, siding up to fears, caving to loneliness. Do not fear your limits, love! Set your course as you know you deserve. Don't settle. You know your worth. Do not pass.

Heard rumors you were asking what I'm like. But no one seemed to know enough to tell. To just ask me yourself would be too risky. So you just moved along to someone else. Always here alone, I remain a mystery. 'Cause it's too much work to find out who I am. No one ever got close enough to start a rumor, so I'm just left to get to know myself.

I miss you in the silent moments in the dead of night when even my thoughts don't quiet the ache of the loss. So much to navigate alone sometimes, I feel like hoisting the black sails on this ship and heading for parts unknown. Were you here, it would still be hard, but not like this. Lament is a vortex I cannot afford to circle, so I press on in hopes I would have made you proud.

I picture you standing motionless, absorbing all the noise around. We are so similar in that respect. Watching and waiting for a moment to slip into a conversation but not really sure how. At times it's exhilarating to be included. A breath of belonging leads to a sigh of relief at a moment of rest. All too fleeting but still sometimes needed before retreating back into the world that we know best.

I saw you thinking about us, in a perfect yesterday. The things we tried so hard to make work, so we could wake together every day. Sometimes it's not that easy, and life gets in the way. But I hold you in my heart. And smile when things look our way.

I thought when I was younger I needed a place I fit. Exhausting to feel alone and seem alright. Soon I found my passion in my solitude, but feeling so deep left me dragging my heavy heart. Some days I wish I could set it all down and run freely. If just for a moment not to have to be strong. But I'm always going to be among the fallen. Making up for the things I feel I should have done.

I'd like to feel the rush of true love someday. I mostly fear the sting of abandonment. No matter how much I want to feel you to be my safe space. A matter of moments can whisk away my belief. I long for rest from the vigilance it takes to trust in another. So I lie down again, alone in the night, cloaked in this blanket of melancholy that has become my truest friend.

If I could touch your heart and feel whether it aches for me, I could then put to rest the worry I'm just not enough for you.

If I ever found the courage to hold your gaze, those steely eyes that I can't ever seem to surprise, I wonder if the comfort they bring would be too much for my bitter heart. I'm afraid of getting lost with you cause you feel like home. So much safer in the dark chambers where I stay, but lonely still when I see you and everything inside me longs to roam.

It's always around, the wonder of belonging but knowing it won't come to pass. Like the solitary life of the raven shining so sleek and dark. Throaty calls deep in the woods while alone it hunts. Some think she has a heart of gold, but they can't know her. She barely knows herself. But slipping back into the darkness she calls home is the closest thing to solace that she's ever known.

I've tried to put into words so many times
what makes me timid and fearful, doubtful of
my way. I know sometimes I seem an
anomaly. The words I'd spill so you could see
where went the boldest parts of me might be
too hard for you to swallow, if I colored them
bold enough for you to glimpse the ruins of
my soul. So I write it off to exulansis and hope
you never have to go where I've been
because you're okay as I hope
to be again.

Parts of me want to be known, and others do not. It's a different combination depending on the day. Sometimes exhausting to feel in control although I know I'm really not. But if you were to really see me, might get more than you were expecting, might shed a tear you didn't see coming, or turn and walk away. So we are so careful and therein lies the problem. Why we don't really know each other; I can't really see you, and you can't see me.

Rainbows have never really been my thing. Give me the hazy greys or the deep inky shadows. A hint of rain and a gentle breeze. Even the power of a storm to weather through. A subtle tinge of darkness to soothe my mood. A chat with the moon before I close my eyes. An achromatic lover has no need for brighter hues to light my way with open eyes.

The best I can do when we are not together is close my eyes and breathe you into my dreams. I feel your deep voice burning through my restlessness, calming the fears of the day that wore me down. Indulgent moments I don't have to be strong until I wake to meet another day without you.

The days melt into one another, and I'm alone again. Trying to catch my breath against a cold wind of sorrow. This is when I close my eyes and lose myself to the woods of my childhood. Lost in a sea of pines and magic on the breeze. The song is so beautiful there. Thousands of teeming small voices singing cause they're free. It's there I find I never was alone again. Just lost amid the bustle, so far from the peace that will ever mean I'm home.

Took some time to sit with my quiet and think about things. My life is filled with notebooks and secrets and not a whole lot else. It's usually a comfort, but sometimes I wonder if I need anything else. Could my day be warmer with someone to share it with? The night is coming, so I'll save that for another day. I smile as I pick up my notebook again.

You see me and the black clouds that shade my face, but instead of seeing me as a curiosity, you come closer. What to do with a soul who takes the time to notice a shadowed life? So many skate by and turn their heads away. Busy being busy and wondering why no one notices when they cry.

You walk by me so many days, and on good days I wonder if you see me. I see you – usually deep in thought, purposefully striding by, a touch of grey at your temples. I often wonder if I captured my voice one of these times to say hello, could I secure your gaze? Would you tell me what you've been thinking about so hard? I brushed past you again today, wishing I could will my heart to try.

You wonder why I never stray from home. I wonder why so many like to roam. I've nothing left for casual or strangers in the void. I'm all in for he who dares to try and touch my very soul. To not be afraid to share their hopes and fears for me to hold. I'm waiting for a home. Anything less, and I'd rather stay completely on my own.

Season of Loss

Dearly departed, the ones who have gone before us, the ones who taught us by example how to live with integrity--how to love when things get tough. My thoughts of them when the breeze catches my hair and makes me grin; such pain of loss of all souls I would gladly bear again and again, just for the grace I feel at having known them and the substance my life would lack if I'd never had the chance.

What I have left of you is in a picture frame. Sometimes I gaze at it, my own face looking back at me, and I wonder--If we'd had more time, would I have to be so strong? Walk through my days, swallowing my uncertainty at who I've become. Some days I lay my weary head on your picture and rest for a moment, and the tears come washing me with new resolve. I've so needed every bit of what I learned from you in our short time. I've needed all the strength I got from losing you. I hope the light you were shining is bright in me, that I touch someone with who I am.

Never have I been able to deal calmly with anyone's passing. How do we release our loved ones to places we cannot fathom? Ashes to ashes is so cold yet somewhat freeing, blowing your body back to the earth where it was made. I will miss your touch and your cheek on mine when we hugged, but a lifetime of love nobody can erase. Your ashes carry through the wind all those places you wanted to go, but your fire can never be quenched, I carry it in my heart wherever I go.

Sat on the porch all night, when it sunk in, you were gone. Tears just leaking down my face. My skin glowing from humidity as I sat and wondered if the weight inside my chest was there to stay? The whiskey almost did not burn. I always thought you'd be back. Until the sunfire dawn broke over the water, and my first day arrived that would never have you in it.

Thoughts of a strong woman today, who took me to be family as if I had been hers all along. Ever straightforward. The compassion was in her; honest to say what you needed, not just wanted. One influence who showed me daily that I could thrive alone was strong enough to face whatever comes. Were I to touch half the lives she has, I would feel it had meant something to be me.

Rest easy.

Thank you for loving me.

We never know the moment, or hour our loved one is no longer entrusted to our care. There are no words for the pain or understanding how we will function again. In my days of loss, the only comfort I can see is my God holding vigil over me. I'll always see them in the moments I feel most alive. I'll come to feel stronger knowing they watch over me. The counsel I gave them was enough; they knew my love. My God needed them so much more up above.

Season of Love

I see your reflection sometimes in the things I do, choices I make, that little extra push I need to take a leap. We don't always have what it takes in moments, but I can carry some of you in my heart. I always thought you were stronger, but who carried you?

I see the strength in you, always giving, always pushing, even when the days are tough. I admire the way you make the best of things when I'd want to bolt and run. You can't know how you inspire me to be better, stronger, how I'm waking up to a better version of myself. You just give--that's what you do. And I hope someday you can see who I see behind those tired eyes I love.

I often think I'd love to luxuriate in the thought you could feel for me, flaws and all-- tattered soul dragging through the mud like a battle flag, and you don't see me that way. What would it be like to accept that as truth? To let you care for me as you see me and not as I see myself? It's a terrifying prospect and one I hope to tackle someday. For now, let me rest my weary head on your broad chest and fall asleep to the sweet sound of a heart that could beat for me.

I heard what you said
Let it sink into my bones
I dared hope to live

The way is you see me
I wish I could reconcile
I see mere shadow

Been a while since I could look up in the bruised evening sky and not drift to thoughts of you. Alone with my mind, you're like a persistent burn that just won't heal. I don't mean that in the way you think. It's a flush to my skin and an awareness of the heat, no matter what I'm doing. You always did know me best. If I could stop thinking of you, I don't know if I would. Everyone needs a fire to call home.

And what do I know of love, really? It's a lonely garden choking on its own weeds. Not sure how to pluck the things that hurt it. Were it free to roam the trellises and walks, would it feel exposed and afraid? It's a balancing of what you feed and nurture. The heartier specimens don't need special care, but the exquisite strains require your attention, or to dust you'll soon find your precious beauty there. What then do I know of love? Maybe not enough to stay in my lonely garden.

All the things I'd love to share with you get bottled up inside my throat, constricted by my fears. I'd like to think you'd love to hear the waves of my feelings for you, but we both know I don't have the strength to say what you need to hear. So I'll write letters to the ocean when you leave and maybe on some shore one day all I feel will be revealed; washed ashore with the tears from my heart that beats for you still.

A storm is coming. I can feel the coolness of it in the wind, the misty air clinging to my skin. It's been here before. Rumbling, crackling, lighting up the dark sky but only for the briefest moments. So still, I am comforted in the dark. So unstable when the air masses meet and oppose the feel of each other. Yet wash everything new after the violence of you. I feel a storm coming.

It is just magic, the way his eyes can calm my weary soul. I didn't trust the storms within them for so very long, but the peace I feel inside me when he holds me without question dares me to think it's possible I found myself a home.

★ · ✦ · ★

In my ardent dreams,
I still never saw you coming.

I'm waiting around for a certain kind of love. In the waiting, I find more of me and what I need. I'd like to be first in your thoughts when you wake and sleep. The one you call because you know you can count on me. Spent a lot of time living way down at the bottom of someone else's life; it's not for me. I deserve to be every bit as important as you'll be to me.

I'm no stranger to melancholy. It's woven into my veins and has always belonged. It's the hint of mirth that leaves me now bewildered. Like a fog, it settles in when I'm with you. I'm spelled by the calmness your touch elicits. I dare to dream that maybe what I am and what you bring could coexist within this fractured hopeful heart of mine.

I want to be the one you come to when things get too much alone. Hate feeling like you need to shelter me from the dark you have to shoulder. I know I'm not easy either, holding pain in little chambers within. What would happen if we walked there together? Hope the fear of trying won't stop us from knowing that kind of love.

I try so hard to put into words the feelings I have for you, so you can know. I know it's important, but that makes it worse cause I don't want to mess it up. Sometimes I feel like watching my mind wrestle with my heart is like a train wreck; you just can't look away. Before it's too late, I hope I get it right or maybe just in knowing me, you already do.

I've exhausted all the reasons to push you away. Worn and weary from running in fear of the sting of love. You could take my heart in your hands, crush it once again, and I'd still close my eyes to remember how it felt for a moment, when the song you placed in my soul was a symphony of everything I needed it to be.

I think of all the ways that you've been there
for me. Things I refused to notice at the time.
Things I pushed to back corners in my mind. I
never wanted to see myself as needing what
you offered. It's too dangerous to brush aside
the cobwebs of my heart to let you in. Now I
feel a shiver at the thought of ever missing
anything you've brought.

That thing you do--protecting those who can't do it themselves, talking to the one in the room sitting alone, a million little choices in the moments of your day. Consistently selfless. Everyday hero, with a huge grin, but you don't notice, it's just who you are, and it is everything.

My mind wills me to stop, but my heart opens up to you like a racing current that's found its ground; no way to stop the path once it's been started. I just hope when my feelings are released, after all this time, it won't be enough to burn us both to ashes.

Thought I loved the silence
until you spoke my name.

I often picture you walking alongside us, telling a story. Never just a story but something we needed to learn. You appear to be so austere from first glance but the witty and even serious moments that break your face into a grin always make me lighter. You always know my heart, even weighted by your own struggles. Ever my fondest champion and example of the meaning of true love.

Moments in my mind; reminders of the days I spend with you. Although my words are shaky and don't often find my voice, the rhapsodic hum coursing through my veins plays just for you--the unspoken testament to what you do. My wish is that you feel my pulse beating all the warmer by your side.

So many things run through me as I wonder how to say all you mean to me. I think of the painful lessons we had to learn along the way to becoming who we are. Often times a yawning hole opened up inside me whenever you were hurting. No amount of fixing could ever show the regret I carry for just not being better. I love the way you pick yourself up and dust off the doubts, pick up your head, and keep going. Your gift has always been that gait, carrying yourself away from things meant to harm. The depth of love I carry, I could just burst. The man you are, you forged yourself, and nothing can ever take away that weld.

Know you get tired sometimes from the weight of all you carry. When the time comes, you can't hold up your walls alone anymore; I'll still be here. Just run to me. There will be no need for questions or even answers. Just help to hold you up before you fall. I know it'd be the last thing you would want. It can always be our little secret. Until you're strong enough to go on, run to me.

No matter what happens in the end, love lingers here. I did what I could to make you whole. You accepted what I gave in the ways that you are able. Things don't always go as we plan, but they are no less noble for how they end. Love lingers here.

I miss your gaze scorching my soul.

Season of Night

I can feel the darkness pool around me as midnight rolls around. It's almost like the air crackles with excitement at the heavy silence; the time of day I feel most alive. My blood hums in my veins like the sad song the crickets bring when the lights grow dim. The solitude comforts my weary soul and lightens my load for a few dusky moments to renew my soul for the next coming day.

And the darkness will always be my home.
Calmest am I in the coolest blanket of night,
surrounded by a conspiracy of ravens singing
their haunted melody and the creatures who
feel the bravest undercover coming out to
roam freely by the moonlight, so much like
me. It's hard for me to see. Who would not
feel comfort it by an inky pool of midnight?

Always too much or too little. Never sure why I bother to even try. "I'm known to be quite vexing" sounds captivating until you delve into my chambers. Were you to find my melancholia appealing, how long to you found the novelty of me lacking? So see me walking by and fading into the mist of night. I am home there, and you need more.

I don't fear the demons that I encounter through my nights. I'm just still long enough for them to say what I don't want to hear and the ghosts of my past; I'm so glad they're no longer real. Just the mirage for haunted memories I can visit and then leave. In my darkest hours, from dusk until dawn, they don't take up the space that they used to. My darkness is my friend. I don't have to let them in. I spend my nights now smiling at the moon and reveling in the thoughts that nothing back there bested me.

And when I see the night sky glowing with stars and feel the cool breeze thick through the darkness, I can breathe and close my eyes for just a moment. The fear I feel in the day grows so small, just like a pinprick. Reminding me it's there but not in control. I hold these respites close to my heart, recharging me for the day that lies ahead, and dream of the night to come to help me make it through another, a little brighter than the one before.

And I wander through these days, plans in place to bring me back when I drift away. There's a soulful darkness deep within the chambers of my heart, so familiar it is my comfort that draws me away from who I want to be; makes the silence sting with insecurities, how I long for a flicker of flame to bring me back those nights that I wander.

And if you find that place that soothes your
heart, makes the days seem bearable,
changes less daunting, don't lose sight of it.
Make it your secret to tuck away when you
need to just be. I find comfort in the night;
still, pooling darkness, bitter quiet. What is it
for you? We all need a place to
truly be ourselves.

Almost dusk, and I can feel the night coming alive. Draws me in with blurred lines and cool breezes I know reach deep into the sky, and I wonder what they say about you seeing the same sky as mine. So far away, yet so close to my heart. Maybe that's why I've always been a stargazer. Wishing you close enough to brush my cheek with the kiss of winds in the dusk as the stars twinkle like that light you get in your eyes. I trace the lines in my sky and remember you.

My life is lived in shades of grey. Not much need have I for color, as I crave the darkness of the shadows, the cool and soothing balm it brings to my broken soul. I wonder sometimes what it would be to live in black-and-white. I feel the absolutes would bring too much for me to bear, forever confounded by what I'd think I was

meant to be.

Lying in the inky black silence, waiting for my thoughts to stop spinning, I will the quiet to seep into my mind. I feel my vulnerability like a sting to my cheek, and I long for a breeze to chill the heat of tears. Were I rough like a stone or stoic as a raven, at last, I could rest and not leave behind pieces I need. For now, I'll gather what is left and drift to the night symphony.

It's the little things that make the night my comfort. The obscure glow from the sky just shy of midnight. The slight chill after humidity has gone to rest. The blanket of humming silence that sets my soul to rest. The haunting of a night owl, a lone soul awake way past the gloaming. The night sings a song for those like me.

★ · ◆ · ★

It's 3:00 a.m. again, and I am awake, scrolling through my thoughts. The only time I really feel like myself; while the world sleeps, sitting in my pool of darkness where I am energized by the silence. It's 3:00 a.m., and I sigh a breath of relief because for a few moments, I can be just me.

In the calm of the night, I can breathe, an inky black shroud of peace surrounding me. So many possibilities for me I can't embrace in the noise and brightness of the day unless it's grey. Some of us are made that way. Lying here in the dark, with the hint of a smile, I can see glimpses of a future built for me, and I'm at peace. The darkness recharges my soul with hope, so I'll be ready come tomorrow.

I see people so differently from you. Probably why we just couldn't get along. We all have our crosses to bear, but you judge from the outside, never waiting to see the glowing soul under the layers of dust and defeat, wearing your shameless halo and missing the gift of those that live in a shadow. So sorry you won't get to see the beauty in the ones you dismiss cloaked in darkness just like me.

I dreamed of the day my solitude would free me. I feel the lone within me no matter where I go, but some weren't made to walk that close to others or have the strength to meld with everyone else. I could try my best to give what you wanted, but you can't give away what you lack inside yourself. So I'll be grateful for moments I made you smile and carry them back to my darkness for the longer nights.

Night air tinged with dew

Crickets sing a lullaby

Stars comfort my soul

When sadness cloaks me

I shore up for the gloaming

The night is my friend

I get the ones that fear the dark, though I never could. My constant companion throughout my life, the one steady thing I know. It pools around me inky black and cloaks me in its depths. And once you feel the chill of it, you're hard-pressed to come back. Soothing, striking, so complete, I feel at home in the silence. Maybe one day, I will venture out. Until then, all the shades feel like magic.

The night envelops me like a long-lost friend. I
wait all day for the stillness it brings; soothes
like the cheerful song of the black sparrow.
And the moon electric in its glow tingles in my
blood, and the words flow. They calm the
beast within me for a time, so I may rest my
weary mind in the darkness I
have taken as my own.

The night calls to me, and I can't sleep, remembering who I have been, thinking of who I'd like to be, not sure if I'm ever-changing or ever the same. What will it be today, violets and voodoo dolls? I run all the ends of the spectrum. I wonder, should I find a place in me called home, should I still roam? I think maybe I was just made to wander.

Some days seem like so much time has passed before I look up to see the setting sun. Things that drain our souls and try our resolve to keep pressing forward; pain of loss, heartache, indecision, leach the fire right out of me. There's another day coming on the horizon, another chance to make it right. I sit in the night looking for meaning, waiting to get up and begin once more.

On beautiful days like this, I can almost embrace the thoughts of figments and fairy tales. Sun on my face and love in my heart, a place to go that's warm and bright, but that for me is not quite right. I was made to embrace the night, and as cold and damp it may seem to be, the darkness still, it comforts me.

You come to me after twilight; I can barely breathe, waiting for my dreams to conjure you. It's raining roses in my mind, the darkest ones to match my cold heart. Were you not a visage I dreamed, I'd likely leave you standing there, but in the dark of night, I'm safe from my despair that haunts me in the daylight and keeps me company when the stars come alive.

Nights you feel so many different emotions coursing through your mind. These are the ones so hard to sort, so you can find some rest; the feelings well within me, and I have to bleed them out somehow. Overflowing onto the page before a dam cracks in my walls. I seek shelter behind them, though my eyes catch some light from outside. One day I hope to venture out when my heart is not too heavy to hide.

Nights like these alone with my thoughts, my feelings can just go either way. I carry so much within me that cries for attention; it's hard to set it down and catch a breath. Nights like these that I'm in awe I can feel peace and a smile trying to curl my lips. If you could be here now, you'd be surprised how far I've come. I think it myself, alone and not afraid most days. Setting down my doubts for a moment just to enjoy finding out who I am becoming.

The time came again when I find out that you found a better one. More sparkly, less dreary, charismatic? I've forgotten all the ways. I even find it eerie that I don't care more. I'm energized and alone again in the moonlight. Soothed by the things that make me this way. I'll be content in the languid darkness until the bitter sun's arrival, and I'll close the chamber door again to protect
my weary heart.

When I dare, I dream and shades of grey; my favorite muted tones that calm my soul. Sometimes I can go on and form a semblance of timid plans before the spell is broken, a future of hope far away from the ruins of my past. I don't regret my path at all because it forged this fire within me, but when I dream, I can loosen my shackles, I can shrug what weighs me for a moment and feel the hint of a grin; I feel light and almost happy when I dream.

This welling inside me just can't be extinguished. Some things have tried, but I rise up once again. I'd love to soar the sky like a Chiroptera--feelings to guide me and breezes to ride across the blackest of nights; something so odd and misunderstood, capable of spreading such good. The parts of me only a few can touch burn the brightest when held with a care that's borne of trust.

There's a stirring in my mind as the sun goes down. The world drifts off as everything in me comes to life. Always been this way, and on the bad nights, I pray for silence in a heart and mind that never stops its turning. Even in my small victories, it questions what I've done, reminds me that it thinks I'm not enough. But I am. And you are. And each day, another chance to wish for a sweet silence when it no longer has a reason to hold me down. What a beautifully quiet day that will be.

Wish some long dark nights that trusting someone were not so alien to me. I wander the halls, stare out into the night. That typically comforts me, but on those nights, I feel no rest. A gentle sigh, the brush of lips on my forehead, these creature comforts I've so long lived without, make me feel like a stranger in this world that loves so freely. So I sit, waiting for another dawn
of hope--tomorrow.

Season of Rising

I saw myself today. Not who I try and think I am. Not who I think you think I am, just me. It was rather curious at first. I stood, assessing, staring, cocking my head. Was it me? And then it just was. A sigh of acceptance and a promise to myself to keep moving forward. I saw myself today, and it wasn't the horror I thought it would be. I kinda was proud of her anyway--me.

In the quiet, I can think of all the days that have gone on before me. Some I feared I'd never make it through. Been broken, joyful, decimated, and in awe. The ride has not been easy but gave me depth. My only regret would be when I felt unworthy. Some moments too great or full of loss to comprehend. I'm not for everyone, but I am strong. Feeling everything has kept me grounded and soaring through the stars.

It comes for me some nights--the feeling I've been here before. Words and opinions once hollow have become something to question as I learn to trust myself again, as I remember my worth and my strength. Dusting myself off as I become unchained once more and rise to meet the night with boldness long forgotten.

You always counted me out as among the fallen, never coming down far enough to see what you'd become. Now I'm thriving here in the shadows. And from the pedestal you made yourself, I bet it's cold up there, alone.

The things I feel I fail at over and over, I etch them on my soul like a tattoo. I trace the lines each time I pass that way again and ache over why I'm not better this time. Some days I feel I hold myself down. These flaws etched into me cursed to never be beaten. Maybe I should see them instead as a badge of the things that I am, that have not bested me still. 'Cause I am me, and it's always enough, even on the days I can't see.

On days that look grim, I'm remembering many more I never thought I'd make it through. Yet here I stand, wind on my face and a song in my heart, however melancholy. And the moon will still comfort me tonight and remind me who I am is all right--for me.

My heart's darkness comes only from the shadows I had living in the shade of others. There's a lighter tone of grey these days. As growth begins again in a heart I once thought would cease to beat from all the pain. I soak up the rain and smile at the sun, and my heart gets a little lighter every day I'm left alone to be me.

My soul is housed in a beautiful box, filled with shards and ashes, the remnants of my memories, the promise of who I'd like to be. Sometimes I take it out and look inside. A reminder, the things that shaped me didn't break me. It's a testament to my strength when I forget. A beautiful, haunted melody plays whenever I lift the lid, made just to soothe the darkness in my heart.

I've worked so hard all my life to try and be who I should. Rigid rules left me fraught with shame. Inconsistencies left me feeling I'd failed. No one tells you about the delicate balance brought back by playing hard. I'm a woman now; my children are men, and in some ways, I feel I've just been born. I hope to have the courage to reach out and embrace fun and the things that bring wonderment to my parched soul. I want to live with a grin on my face and a song in my heart, long after I'm thought to be old.

I've been guilty before, trying to fit myself inside the image you made of me. Why is it when someone says they love you, it's not you, but who they think you should be? All this breeds in me is misery. So I'm done being anyone you think I (might)could be. There is only one me, and even if I'm never the idea of love for anyone else, as is, it's more than enough just to be me.

You throw everything I give to the ground, so I'm on my knees picking up the pieces. I always had a weakness for the one who dealt the blows. As good as I deal to myself, this time, I've been too long without the self-loathing to want to go back. So I rise with the pieces in my hands and shove them back in place, alone, with a grin.

Drinking affirmations at a slow burn doesn't always work for me. Sometimes I feel more inadequate for the wanting. Can I be real in my melancholy and still grow my wings? I believe they might be dark, but they're still mine. Maybe a little scorched but still ready for takeoff. Everyone won't have the same picture of healing, but it's healing just the same. Don't ever let your coping be less. We are all growing the best way we can.

There was a time when it was exquisite madness to try and catch your gaze. So many ways to destroy your soul when you can't see your worth. Tender vines of courage now snake up from a soul on fire and lay yellow poppies near the cold stone of what I once thought I needed. A testament to the woman I've since become.

Finding myself with a little grin, even when things seem scary or a little grim. It's such a strange way to react, but I tend to have hope now like never before. Seeing things through a different lens. One not shaded by confusion or deceit since I've been on my own and away from anyone that makes me doubt my worth. How could I have known it could be so clear without the games you played? Wow, I can't get over how much easier things are and how beautiful. I'd forgotten about me.

I feel change coming, just over the hill. Such a hard thing for me, and I'm never sure why we cling to the familiar sometimes, even though to grow would help so much. Were I able to peep over that hill, I would not be better served because part of the change is the courage it takes to boldly and blindly crest the unknown. So I'll be ready, and I'll own this change with vehemence.

I look pretty put together when I need to make it so. Smart suit pants. Maybe some jewelry. Don the war paint. But that same little girl is quaking in her suave attire. Peeking from behind a lock of long hair at the power suits in the room, wondering if today would be the day I falter on the outside, and I'll be seen as the girl I feel I am on the inside. Would that be so bad anyway? Guess we will wait and maybe see--someday.

Walking through my memories is often painful, so I avoid the chore. But what about the beautiful ones destined to die and fade to grey because I had a few bad days, or years, or months? Some silly tiny happy things in those days were the glue that held me together. Don't they deserve to be archived in the brightest place of my mind? So shame on me when I shut my mind to my past. Those brief moments of bliss carried me, made me what I am today, and they are everything.

★ · ◆ · ★

This road I find myself on it seems to change every few days. I like to think I'm grounded, so I feel a little security, but actually, I'm a traveller, moving on when I dare to make things better. Wandering at least in my mind, hoping to find some peace for my weary soul, daring to try again, and again for happiness and a home--just a traveler.

Those times when my mind takes long passages through things that have come to pass, I can feel the silence I've tried to give those that couldn't choke out the words they felt; the deep bone ache of losses that revisit from time to time. The things I'm at peace with, I never thought I'd survive. I close my eyes and feel the breeze across my weary soul, and have to smile. For all the moments have brought us to where we are, and no matter the setting, this time is perfect. For who we have become is still unfolding.

There's a part of you who knows how to get through those days. The ones where you ache and the time drags on forever. It's the same part of you that can finish rep 13, 14, 15 when your body says you have nothing left. We forget we have it. We don't need it as often as it feels like we do, but it pulls us through. You can always count on you.

Season of Wonder

And what do I really want, for me? So many years, I thought I knew. So many choices made based in fallacy. Disillusioned by the pretty words I thought I wanted to hear by men who never tried to know me. I was wrong, and now I know. When I look out at the night sky, and I am whole, not longing for completion, what I needed has been within me all along.

And what if I could say to you the things you've been longing for me to say? Would it make them mean more? Sometimes the feelings burst up from my chest but snag right there in my throat. I wonder, do you feel the same? What will you think? Why does it matter? We still feel it. Love is bold. Love takes a risk. These are the things that make it worth loving you.

And what if I were to tell you the things you do that give me strength? Would you even believe you had a hand in holding me up at all? To see me from outside, I may look like I have it all together, but sometimes inside, I'm a puddle, losing bits of me through the cracks. I need someone to believe in me as so often that one isn't me. Were I to dare trust in what you think, would it bolster faith in myself? Guess we'll go along day-to-day and see how it plays out eventually.

Fire and ice, I hold them both within me. Mostly my mind is aflame with wonder and passion for what I think I love or need. My heart is much more stoic, quenching the flames when I dive without caution, bringing me back to the cold of reality. How they pull me back and forth is fascinating. Were they ever to balance, I'm afraid I would never experience this beautiful contradiction that is me.

Had a burst of fun without the usual judging of myself, and it was almost surreal. Can you really feel good about yourself whenever you want? Paint yourself beautiful and live in the moment without care? I wish we could all get this, even for a moment. So many things to weigh us down; it's hard to hit pause and take a breath, but you can, and it's magic.

I hear what you used to say in lost whispers of days gone by; before things seemed so hard, people began lashing out to not be hurt first. When we were real and said what we felt. Younger days when I felt so right because it meant a lot to say, "I've got your back." And the words were spoken you needed to hear without expecting anything back. I miss it, the raw honesty from lost whispers of you.

I see the way you look at me, almost into me, and I often wonder what you see. I spend so much time in my own thoughts; it's curious to think of sharing them with another. And would you walk away? And would I welcome it? Alone drifting dreamily through the darkened rooms I've built in the chambers of my heart. This melancholy has been my constant for so long it breeds comfort within my veins. The thought of sharing my dreams with you brings a flush to my cheek, and is that hope unfurling in my chest? One day maybe I will let myself see what you see and take that chance.

It's a metamorphosis I have to go through just to entertain the thought of letting you in. I know that seems dramatic, and if there were a way to heal my fragmented heart, I would truly let you in. But at what cost? My instant gratification wants someone to fill the void, but my everlasting heart desires someone to stay the course. Therein lies my dilemma; am I worth it to you?

Never feel quite steady enough to take off
from the ground. I dream of black wings
soaring high, manipulating the wind to carry
me through the darkest skies. No longer to
scrape the ground, head down, with my fears
at the ready but a battle cry working up
through my body to burst out hope of a
stronger me ahead. As I drift past the moon,
on light warm breezes and memories of
how it felt to be secure in me.

Picket fences don't get the respect they deserve. Nostalgia. A lost childhood. Peeling paint and dry wood capturing moments of tears and laughs. A sign of strength and stability. An easier time before things became so hard. Were my life wrapped in an old picket fence, maybe I'd have the courage to grow into me.

Some days I wonder about the icy blood in my veins and what the color might be. Some we bleed onto the paper. It's a relief to think it's all inside; if I don't want you to see. Not always cathartic to spill it. Sometimes, I've carried the weight so long it's become like an old friend. I wish I wrote only because I want to, but some things just look less tangled on paper while I dress the wound and color the words to look pretty to be read.

Some days it's hard to see the wreckage left inside me as a beautiful disaster like the poets say. Other days there's a tiny fire burning in my gut, sparking me on, edging me ever closer to feeling like myself again. And that me, it's okay to want to be. Would it be so bad to embrace who you are? Those who want you to be something different, they will never be satisfied with the beauty that you bring. But you can, and I can be, the beautiful disaster we were always meant to be.

Some nights I wander through the halls of my mind and ponder stacks of statues I've picked up along my way. Were I not bound by these seemingly unbreakable walls, could I carve out a life uniquely made for me? Were there no rules I've placed on my own personality, what kind of life would that be? Less rigid, fearful, compliant, shy; maybe we would all like to see who I would be--a little bit more like me.

The things that trap me in my day-to-day, what would it be to languish a while without their weight? Always too responsible, I've come to snuff out the very idea of play. I long for a span of time without a care but to laugh so hard it brings tears. What could really happen, loving without the reservation we feel so necessary for protection? Would that be so ruinous? I'd like to see, if only for a few precious moments, what it would be like to be free.

The way you hold yourself together is quite a show to those who don't know the secrets you hide that cause you to feel so terrible. I sometimes think the exquisite pain this causes you is maybe a drug in itself. Why else would you choose to endure it another day? I hope one-day peace finds you when you're not afraid of it. So you can ease into a better place and rest your weary head.

Thought of you today. Wonder where you'd be without chasing ghosts and rearview mirrors to light your way. My wish would be you'd see there's nothing left behind but the way you thought it would be, and that's not really worth chasing; it never really was. Like to see you riding off with a smile towards a dream that takes you forward. Don't look back. You can be brave. I believe in you.

What kind of courage would it take to love again? I see people talk about it so freely. Yet, for me, it has always caused harm. When what you crave causes you the cavernous pain that renders you listless, how can you pursue a chance to be happy and cherished? My soul beats searching for the rhythm of another. So I'll press on in hopes one day I'll find what I deserve--in spite of me.

You don't know me. Sometimes you act like you do, feigning concern for things you think about me. How much more of your time would it take to just ask? I have feelings. I see you watching me like I'm a mystery. Maybe think I'm strong, and you want to be. If you knew the things that rage inside me, you might change your mind. But we won't know, will we? Cause I am here, and you stay there, and you can't get to know me cause then I wouldn't be a mystery.

About the Author

Dawn P. Harrell calls Southern Mississippi home where she works full-time and loves being outside. She cherishes spending time with her two grown sons, her daughter-in-law, and three rescue dogs.

A writer by hobby, she started sharing her writing at the encouragement of several friends, and in 2018 Dawn created a Facebook page, aptly named, Seasons of a Sewer Girl.

Her writing comes from experience, and much of it tends to have a darker feel, but that's because the words are her journey, her truth. Dawn doesn't try and hide her scars. She puts them out there for all to see. Dawn shares her vulnerabilities and most intimate thoughts to let others, who may have experienced abuse or have struggled with self-worth, know they are not alone.

Dawn is shamelessly nerdy, a longtime lover of the night, and when she's not working or writing, you can find her at 3 a.m. looking at the stars and contemplating her next written piece or watching classic horror movies.

If you would like to follow or connect with Dawn, please visit: https://linktr.ee/DawnPHarrell

Made in the USA
Middletown, DE
10 May 2022

65575743R00132